A RHYME IN DUE TIME

A Rhyme in Due Time

Deborah M. Borchelt

Deborah M. Borchelt

XULON PRESS

Xulon Press
2301 Lucien Way #415
Maitland, FL 32751
407.339.4217
www.xulonpress.com

© 2019 by Deborah M. Borchelt

All rights reserved solely by the author. The author guarantees all contents are original and do not infringe upon the legal rights of any other person or work. No part of this book may be reproduced in any form without the permission of the author. The views expressed in this book are not necessarily those of the publisher.

Printed in the United States of America.

ISBN-13: 978-1-5456-7975-3

CONTENTS

A Cry For Help 1
A Letter to Heaven 2
A Plea From a Child of God 4
A Prayer For the Lost 6
A Time. 7
A Tribute to Our Parents Elmer & Martha Crocker 8
A Vessel. 11
ABC's of Salvation 13
All About Our God 14
Angels. 17
Anger. 18
Better Together 21
Borrowed Time 23
Children. 25
Crossing Over 26
Dear God. 27
Death 29
Dedication Poem. 31
Dreams 32
Father God. 33
Fear 35
Freedom 37
Habits and Addictions. 38
Hardships 41
Heaven 43
Homeless. 45

I'm Coming Again 46
Judgement Day We All Must Be Ready to Heed the
    Father's Call 48
Just In Case 51
Let Go & Let God 53
Life 54
Love Is 55
Love 57
Marriage Prayer 59
Miracles Of Jesus 61
Miracles... 62
Mother.. 63
Father 65
My Baby Angel..................................... 67
My Special Friend.................................. 69
Open 70
Our Church 72
Prayer 74
Sounds Like Heaven 75
Starting Over...................................... 77
Still Time For You.................................. 79
Teardrops... 81
Thankful 83

DEDICATION

This book is a special dedication for my family, friends and any who struggle with our common everyday issues. Life revolves around many obstacles both good and bad. It's my hearts desire that these will help and encourage you. Even in the most simplest form they drive home and create a strong message that can far outweigh any onslaught from the enemy.

My prayer is for this book to become a useful tool and to spread like a virus. I'm hopeful that it will deliver comfort and a way to connect or move you closer to God.

A Cry for Help

How do I value a human day life
when all that I have are pains toil and strife

I look for the answer in the eye of another
with a sorrowful heart I turn to my mother

I am struggling down a long weary road
with all I can carry it is quite a load

My life is not perfect at a certain point of view
my troubles are many my worries are too

I am always in a quest fighting for
survival to pass my life's test

I may have a history of falling short
I have a strong will to give it my best
with an open mind and heart

I don't say these things for sympathy
but for encouragement love and strength I need

Forgive me and help me is my feeble plea
I need some help and sanity

I know there is hope for me in everything I do
because of my lifelong struggles I have found this to be true

A Letter to Heaven

Although there is a distance that keeps us apart
You'll always have a place within my heart
It's so hard to believe how long it has been
the clock keeps on ticking time keeps moving on

I sure do miss talking to you and all
of the other fun things we used to do
I miss your pretty smile and brushing your hair
I wish you were still here

I know that you're in a better place
I know you're no longer in any pain
at times my heart cries out for you
I still love and miss you just the same

A Letter to Heaven

The last five years for me
have been the very best
I 've received a special calling
I'm up for my first test

I have come to realize through
many of my ordeals
that these have equipped me
for what I'm about to do

I can stand on my own two feet again
proud of who I am
I recognize and accept the fact
that these were not in vain

PS Love Always
I remember how fond you were of poetry
This book is for you

A Plea from a Child of God

Please break these
    addictions that are
keeping me from
being as close to you
that I need to be

The weight is so heavy
I just need to let go
The distance is far
I need you so

It doesn't matter to you
the things I have done
For you have been great
and excused every one

A Plea From a Child of God

Your expectations
are high I know
I can do this
If only I would try

The name of Jesus has
so much power
Never the devil
can ever devour

Help me Dear Lord
to put these away
Hold me so close
that I will not stray

A PRAYER FOR THE LOST

*H*elp me don't hurt me I have feelings too
I want to change and rearrange the ways
I've always used

If and when I fall please help me to rise
please hold me tight don't let me go
I need you so

Help me to always consider you first so
I'm not left to struggle alone throughout
the worst

Many a friend has paid the horrible cost
how unfortunate for those who are
forever lost

Help us Dear Father
in all that we do
Lead us to those
who don't know you

                          Amen

A TIME

There is a time for everything

A time to be born   A time to die
A time to laugh   A time to cry
A time for peace   A time for war

A time to give thanks for
what they fought for

A time to crawl   A time to walk
A time to listen before you talk
A time to walk   A time to run
A time to be serious   A time to have fun

A time for me   A time for you
May we blessed our
whole life through

A time to kneel   A time to pray
A time to Thank God
for each and everyday

A TRIBUTE TO OUR PARENTS
ELMER & MARTHA CROCKER

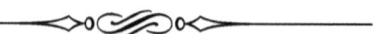

Our Mother and Father
   A Classic Christian duet
For all that you've done for us
we never will forget
You always shared your faith
and let your voice be known
Always full of confidence that
We were going to know Our Lord
over time our faith in Him
and love for Him
would surely grow
You took us to church
twice on Sunday
in the middle of the week
on a Wednesday
teaching us life's lessons
with examples for us to follow

A Tribute to Our Parents Elmer & Martha Crocker

All of your consistency over the years
has gotten us through some many ordeals
Thank you Mom and Dad for your love
patience and guidance too
We might all be lost if we
didn't have parents like you
Until that Chosen Day when
we shall finally reunite
We will carry you in our hearts
and our Memories close in sight
Love Always
Linda Mary Mike Winston
Mark Rick Debbie and Vicky

A VESSEL

Let me be a chosen vessel
   for you Dear Lord I pray
There are many souls in the midst and
stranded in sin along the bays
Let your words be their inspiration
to gently turn this ship around
Back to the big wide sea
We are homeward bound
Cast our nets wide open
to gather others along the way
We know there are others out there
who are struggling on their way
With your guidance and direction
Lord allow them to understand to
follow their heart's desire
to become Good Godly men
Your knowledge is our power
we are forever humbled in your debt
You fill us with your Holy Spirit
we honor you with our respect

ABC'S OF SALVATION

ADMIT WE ARE SINNERS
BELIEVE BE BAPTIZED
CONFESS OUR SINS
DELIVER US FROM EVIL
EDIFY THE CHURCH
FAITH THE SIZE OF A MUSTARD SEED
WE ARE SINNERS SAVED BY **G**RACE
MY **H**ELP COMES FROM THE LORD
GOD MADE MAN IN HIS OWN **I**MAGE
JUDGE NOT LEST YE BE JUDGED
KNOW THE TRUTH
LOVE THY NEIGHBOR AS THYSELF
MEDITATE ON MY WORD BOTH DAY AND NIGHT
NEW NAME IN CHRIST JESUS
KNOCK AND THE DOOR WILL BE **O**PEN
IN ALL THINGS WE SHOULD **P**RAY
BE **Q**UIET BEFORE THE LORD
BRING **R**ESTORATION TO MY SOUL
SOW THE GOOD SEED
THE **T**RUTH WILL SET YOU FREE
WALK **U**PRIGHT IN THE LORD
VICTORY IN JESUS
HIS **W**ORD DOES NOT COME BACK VOID
I E**X**ALT THEE
YIELD NOT TO TEMPTATION
WE'RE MARCHING TO **Z**ION

ALL ABOUT OUR GOD

Prayer our 911 to Heaven above
    God is never too busy to listen to you
He waits with tender mercy for your
call to come through

God knows our every need
yes each and every one
Whatsoever you ask in my name
for you it shall be done

You don't have to wait for
a special time of day
Whenever you need him just
Pray pray pray

God cannot tell a lie
He is unchangeable without a doubt
You just take him at his word
you will never be without

All About Our God

God is the same yesterday today and forever
He cast out his love and care
His angels keep watch over us
for times of trouble and despair

God is patient loving and kind
even when we sin and fall short
If we only repent
He remembers them no more

Consider him first in
all that you do
God will make straight
the path for you

ANGELS

Angels are among us
each and everyday
They watch over us
to lead us out of harm's way
Angels can be with us
we may not even know they're there
We can feel and sense their presence
for we know that he doth care
Angels are Gods Special Messengers
sent from Heaven up above
They give us special mercies
out of His caring tender love
Angels are a light of glory
thus to lead the way
For they do and keep his will
each and every day
For God loves us so much
more than we can know
He knows our every step
before we even go

ANGER

My name is anger
I have no reproach
or shame I will fester
up inside you with only
you to blame you'll
have to move much faster
if you think you'll catch me
I can run just like a tiger
or snap just like a pea
No one can ever stop me
so don't you even try
I will torture and entangle you
without any reason why
My mind is full of fury
My fists are full of rage
My lips speak a brutal language
they better lock me in a cage
My anger brings out the worst

Anger

in me and puts me to the test
I can make life so difficult
who cares about the stress
I blame my faults on others
I don't have any self-respect
I'm direct to the point
sometimes very rude
I keep riding the same vicious cycles
what else is there to do
I don't always stop to think
about the actions that I take
I just suffer from the agony
of what might happen next

BETTER TOGETHER

Better together
never to part
Two lives to grow
sharing their hearts
Consumed with Love
in all they do
Excusing each weakness
they are put through

Let respect and honor
always be your guide
With tenderness and mercy
In each other you confide
Never let the sun go down
and be angered
Make your amends quickly
don't let it linger

Always be willing to forgive
For this is how we are to live

BORROWED TIME

I feel like I'm living on borrowed time
I feel like I'm living on borrowed time
God is so good to me
but I feel like I'm living on borrowed time

I've so much to finish
I pray to get it all done
to leave a chosen legacy for
those that are yet to come

I have learned to be content
sometimes without even a dime
The struggles are real but
I live one day at a time

I feel so overtaken
by his mercies and his love
For he knows my every need
yes each and everyone

The clock it just keeps ticking
my heart is growing weaker
When I think it might be soon
God keeps giving me borrowed time

CHILDREN

Children are special blessings
    sent from God in Heaven above
Children are conceived by us
out of love

As newborn babes
require so much care this
we shall be giving
with much more to share

We tend to each need every single one
for they cannot do no such one
They crawl then they walk
they steal your heart
When they start to talk

As they grow how quickly the time goes by
your sweet little babe has grown into a child
With so much ahead of them to learn and do
They will be around many others
who may not be just like you

We must teach our children
to listen pray and always obey
They shall make us happy and
not put us to shame this is the
guidance of which they became

CROSSING OVER

Just crossed over to my new
  Home with no more tears or
sorrow or any need to roam

The streets here are paved
of gold the people here
they just never grow old
The rooms here are many with
numbers untold

The angels sing a sweet melody
It truly sounds just like a symphony
now reunited with my family
and friends our time here
Will never end

I can't wait for you to see it
you won't believe your eyes
This breath taking beauty
A Mansion in the Sky

DEAR GOD

Sometimes we struggle
    sometimes we fight
Because each of us feel
we have to be right

So to live our lives in harmony
we must pray together and agree
For this was all part of God's wonderful plan
and so he took the rib from man

Now to make this man complete
He caused him to fall into a deep sleep
for God did not want man to be alone
He should have a helper
one he can lean on and call his own

I know it's not so easy to live in harmony
If we just have faith the size of a seed
God will move all our mountains
and meet every need In Jesus Name

                          Amen

DEATH

Death is but A knock on Heaven's Door
It's the doorway of Salvation
that has been waiting for you

Death is the result of
what we know to be as sin
A mere passing of this life
to an Eternal One

We'll always grieve and
miss the one we've lost
They will live forevermore
within the memories of our hearts

they are so much better
to be with our Lord
They live in perfect harmony
their days filled with joy

God let us be ready
willing to share
With our hearts and minds
forever being prepared

DEDICATION POEM

I carry my poems with me
   going to and fro
They bring many true blessings
where ever I may go

They are a great source of comfort
for the struggles we must work through
They are God's precious words
for we know these are true

God revealed to me
what I should do
It is my sincere desire
to share these with you

I have lived through many ordeals
I truly believe that is why
I can write these for you

My prayer for any of you
that will read them through
That you will be blessed
and encouraged too

DREAMS

Are what we make of them
they can start kind of scary
Then turn out really good

We all dream it's as simple as ABC
we close our eyes to sleep
Our mind is the TV

In the still moments
while we are asleep
We can say and do things
you might not even think

What are dreams
the burning desires of our heart or the
Mysteries of our minds
we have no answers for

Dreams are like goals
the things that we aspire to
We long for those missing pieces
to make us feel complete and whole

When you dream
Dream as big as you can
you just never know

What could happen
when you take
the time to plan

FATHER GOD

You are the Potter
I am the clay
Mold me and make me
teach me to pray

Consume me Dear Father
as I continue to grow
Fill my unquenching spirit
to overflow

Lead me Dear Father
the path I should go
Grant me your wisdom
help me to know

Nudge my spirit
to always pray
For I struggle at times
with no words to say

From this day forward
until the very end
Cleanse me and purify me
from all of my sin

I won't allow Satan
To steal me away

FEAR

Persevere and feel your fear
   in fear there is no freedom
It will only bind us up
and keep us needing

Never give up on your
hearts desire keep
the flame burning
like an unquenching fire

Steady your course
hold your head high
Remind yourself I know I can do it
I just have to try

Even if you miss the goal
You are one step closer
and eventually like in golf
You will hit the hole

So persevere
feel that fear
Now do it quickly
your time is here

Don't wait to do
what you hesitate
Convince yourself
Do not procrastinate

FREEDOM

Freedom isn't free
someone fought for
you and me

Many have gone before
fighting for our freedom
in Battles of War

They gave so much
to keep us free to live our lives
as we're meant to be

Freedom comes with an
ultimate price which many
men and women did sacrifice

Even at the
unfortunate cost of
losing their own life

Habits and Addictions

Habits are the strongholds
   of the things we do
We've done them so long
we become addicted to

We all have them
some many some few
They can make you happy
or sometimes make you blue

From smoking to drinking
even drugs of choice too
None of these are good and
most harmful to you

If we are not careful
without even a clue
You could even kill someone
that someone could be you

Habits and Addictions

Even cursing swearing
or unkindness shown
Not any of these
will help his own

There are so many others
we won't name them all
Our lives are full of them
not any of them too small

There are ways to change
if you really want to
You can break the vicious cycles
with much good to do

Get down on your knees
ask God please make you strong
Erase the habits forgive you and to
please take them away

HARDSHIPS

Hardships are God's special
   way of helping us to know
from many a test
we would surely grow

Hardships are a part of life
some many and some few
Count it all a special joy
when hardships fall on you

With all of our griefs and
burdens shared
God will not put on us
no more than we can bear

Heed your ears to listen
to what I've had to say
God's love will surely bless
you every single day

HEAVEN

Oh what a day that will be when our
new homes in Heaven we shall finally see
Where the streets there are paved of gold and
we shall never ever grow old

Oh we're all so anxious for the day
with no more tears to wipe away
For a new immortal body no more pains or
sorrow or even a thought of another tomorrow

Oh what great joy we shall share
when we meet with our loved ones over there
For all the things we've ever wanted to know
God now to us will surely show

Oh what stories we now shall hear
of all the great and wonderful things
We had done while we were there
now we shall live forever here in

Our Beautiful Mansions that God has prepared

HOMELESS

Cries go out in to the night
   some are filled with fear
Fear of the unknown
and fully unaware

In my hours of quietness
In loneliness and despair
So tired, cold, and all alone
it's quite a load to bare

Our lives are so uncertain
we're always on the go
We pray for our safety
to keep moving down the road

It's a temporary stop
waiting for our time to go
We're all just visitors here
this world is not our home

It seems to be the darkest
right before the dawn
I can feel myself now changing
I'm finally going home

I'M COMING AGAIN

I've got a unique story
 for all the world to hear
It's about my friend Jesus
who came to give us life
that freely He did share

God knows that we're not perfect
that's why He sent his son
He was born of the Virgin Mary
no different from our own

Jesus, He was tried and tried
He remained as true
there were many great tasks
set out for Him to do

all of these He did fulfill
so we would know
it was the Father's will

I'm Coming Again

He wants us to be like him
and strive to do our best
to run our race with patience
God will do the rest

Always be watchful
proudly ready to share
He is coming back to get us
the time is drawing near

Jesus, He was crucified for
all the good He
no one even realized
what they had done

In three days He rose again
an empty tomb they did find
God sent His Holy Spirit
Who now reigns from within

JUDGEMENT DAY WE ALL MUST BE READY TO HEED THE FATHER'S CALL

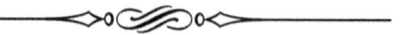

There's a great day coming
   when our lives on earth will be no more
Like a thief in the night He is coming
no one knows the hour
There is no more running
our time has all run out

Every knee will bow
before the throne
and give a full account
The great trumpets will sound
some may fall to death in fear
The skies will open
with Jesus drawing near

Judgement Day We All Must Be Ready to Heed the Father's Call

The sun will no longer rise
The moon will refuse to shine
The stars fall from the sky
A lake of fire and brimstone
is all that will be nigh

The seas will give up their dead and
pour from the shores
All of those that have gone before
will now rise from their graves and live forever more
In the blink of an eye
our bodies will change
We 'll be taken up to heaven
by a rapture in the sky

JUST IN CASE

Just in case you feel the need
   our time is running short
This world is full of craziness
our people are full of greed

We all have a special purpose
a reason to be here
There's someone out there watching
with burdens they don't share

We can't sit by and do nothing
or hope that someone will
We must do something quickly
there is no time to spare

Make sure to lend a helping hand
for those who are in need
Take some lost souls with you
on us their souls depend

LET GO & LET GOD

When we are in sickness
sorrow and pain
Let go and Let God
if you don't the burdens will
rise with much conflict too

When we can't see the light
shining from within
Let go and Let God
Our lights have to shine
for the lost to come in

When the pressures of life
keep pulling you down
Let go and Let God
Have mercy on me Lord
protect me from all harm

When Jesus comes knocking
on your hearts door
Let go and Let God
Give your heart to Jesus
He is the answer to your prayers

When it only takes faith
the size of a seed
Let go and Let God
He will move all your mountains
He will meet every need

LIFE

Life is full of ups and downs
it truly makes the world go round
With so many adventures I have tried
By God's amazing grace
I can hold my head up high

At times the struggles seemed all up hill
with constant sorrow everywhere
With so many bitter yet sweet memories
they have left a lasting impression on me

It hasn't always been easy for me
as I'm sure for others too
Breaking through the vicious cycle
that life can put us through

When the load got so heavy
that I could no longer bear
I gave my life to Jesus
He is the answer

to all of my prayers
In sickness sorrow and pain
He is the one I call upon
Praise His Holy Name

LOVE IS

L	IS FOR THE LOYALTY THAT WE SHALL ALWAYS BE
O	IS FOR THE OPINIONS WE EXPRESS SO OPENLY
V	IS FOR THE VICTORY WE HAVE YET TO SEE
E	IS FOR THE EFFORT PUT FORTH BY YOU AND ME
I	IS FOR INSTITUTE OF MARRIAGE THAT GOD WANTS FOR ME AND YOU
S	IS FOR THE SENTIMENTS OF WHAT WE SAY AND DO

WE KNOW THAT FROM THE BIBLE
GOD TELLS US CLEAR AND TRUE
OF WHAT WE ARE TO SAY AND DO
WITH GOD'S PEACE AND LOVE
THESE THINGS WILL STAY WITH YOU

LOVE

Love will always find you
patient dear and kind
without any envy or be
self-seeking at any time

Love is long-suffering
which means till the end
having no fear or worries
Until all our time is gone

No fits of jealous rage or
unkind words ever spoken
Your love will always guide us
Our oaths will go unbroken

This is what the Lord commands
and this should be our stay
We pray God you will keep us
forever in your way

MARRIAGE PRAYER

We are to Love Honor and Cherish
until Death do us part As we begin our lives
together that We shall be as of one heart

As we begin our journey together down the
long and winding road We will live and learn
from many with numbers untold

Oh God When the storms of life do come our
way and the rains pour too that we shall
always pray and keep our complete trust in you

There will be times We may argue fuss and
fight Our Dear Father God in Heaven always
has a way of making things right

If we can turn these things around with
just a kind word then his love can and
will always abound

We shall keep all of your Commandments and
do our very best to not put each other or You
God to any kind of test

MIRACLES OF JESUS

When Jesus walked the earth for a time
He performed many miracles as a sign
for this was all part of God's perfect plan
to show his unconditional love for man
From changing water to wine
He fed a multitude of many
Jesus healed the sick raised the dead
made the lame to walk and the blind to see
Many were present to witness
the miracles as they came to be
Now throughout time so many
wonderful occurrences they did fulfill
For these were all made possible
because the Father willed
from these things
He acquired many followers too
they were all most faithful
for there was much for them to do
Jesus showed tremendous courage
even to His death on that Old Rugged Cross
He drank that bitter cup of anguish
all of his tasks would soon be finished
The cost of sin is His death
for all of us he did pay
through Christ most perfect blood
Our sins are washed away

MIRACLES

Miracles still do happen
Believe me they really do
at the times you least expect it
Your Miracle will come through
Let Faith and Trust
Always be your guide
and in all matters pray
Follow after Jesus
He is the only way
Keep him first, and foremost
in all that you may do
Count your blessings daily
and show yourself as true
Make sure to keep praising him
in good times and in bad
He will lift you up out of your
trouble He will make you glad
Never give up on your Miracle
it may be arriving to you any day
For these are the things that
can happen when you continue
and not cease to pray

MOTHER

M	IS FOR MARTHA THE SWEETEST PERSON I'VE EVER KNOWN
O	IS FOR THE OPTIMISM THAT SHE WOULD ALWAYS SHOW
T	IS FOR THE THOUGHTFUL THINGS SHE WOULD SAY AND DO
H	IS FOR ALL THE HUGS SHE GAVE THAT ALWAYS SAW US THROUGH
E	IS FOR ENCOURAGEMENT TO ALWAYS KEEP GOING AND TO NEVER QUIT
R	IS FOR THE RESPECT SHE EARNED SHE WAS REALLY QUITE A HIT

FATHER

F   IS FOR MY FATHER WHO PROTECTED AND TOOK CARE OF ME

A   WAS FOR HIS GENUINE USE OF AUTHORITY

T   IS THAT I COULD TRUST HIM WITH ALL OF MY HEART

H   WAS FOR HIS HELPING HANDS TO ASSIST ME WITH MY ART

E   IS FOR ELMER THE ONE THAT I DEPEND UPON

R   IS FOR HIS REWARD MY DAD RESIDES IN HEAVEN

MY BABY ANGEL

How sad was the day when my baby angel passed away
taken in her sleep not even a tear did she weep
It's difficult to cope with the loss of a child
always questioning and wondering why
I rest assured of her care
she has many mommy angels abiding near
My baby angel has a special place and purpose in Heaven
I close my eyes and only imagine
My baby angel in the whitest fluffy wings and gown
I wish I could only hold her now

                In loving memory
              of My Baby Angel
                 Belinda Marie
          May 19, 1983–Aug 19, 1983

MY SPECIAL FRIEND

You were always there for me
through times of thick and thin
I would not dare to smile
or even pose a grin

When times were so hard
you always knew just what to say
How I could keep going
to get me through the day

You have felt my every grief and
hardship you never went away
You were always there to listen and
nudged my heart and spirit to pray

When I could no longer
hold back the tears I cried
You would hold me and console
until I felt better inside

You have done so much for me
I'm sure for many others too
I gladly surrender
my life to you

You'll always be
my special friend
I'll cherish and love you
without any end

OPEN

Open my eyes to see
All of your visions
I need to see

Open my ears to listen
to the messages
I need to hear

Open my mouth to speak
to always pray for
what I need to say

Open my mind
to your ways and
not my own

Open

Open my heart
to love
unconditionally

Create in me your spirit
fill my joy
to overflow

Take away my darkness
show me
the light of day

Take away my weakness
allow me
not to stray

OUR CHURCH

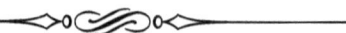

Church is our special family
　　The Body of Believers
of whom we belong
It's our source of strength
we rely and depend upon
With a Pastor
who loves and guides us
the direction we should be in
With the Holy Spirit in charge
we're all sure to win
Our doors are open for all
who will come through
With a warm friendly welcome
a special message from God is
waiting for you

Our Church

With our hands raised to praise
and our knees knelt to pray
Our hearts to you we have given
Our tears and sorrows
go right with them
When Jesus gave his life for us
He set us captives free
Free to choose
our lives with Him
forever free indeed
We are all to spread
the gospel of what
Jesus our Lord had done
That we may be reaching
each and every one.

DEDICATED TO
PARKTON ASSEMBLY OF GOD
IN BARNHART, MO

PASTOR'S MONTY & GLENDA ROARK

PRAYER

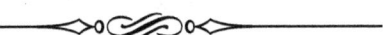

Our Prayers are to
God in Heaven above
We send our prayers to you
with respect and out of love

Our prayers should be spoken in
Faith to the great and mighty one
For God knows our needs
every single one

every day in all
things we should pray
With our faith ever-increasing
thus we shall pray without ceasing

So never hesitate to pray
even if you have lost your way
He is ready and willing to listen to you
for whatever it is you are going through

Know that He is faithful to fulfill
If it is the Father's will
There is so much power in our prayer
if we can only believe that He does hear

SOUNDS LIKE HEAVEN

A life without sorrow no pain or worries
or money to borrow A brand new body
that needs no fixing A promise of Eternal Life
that is truly a blessing

No more time clocks to punch or traffic jams to sit-in
No more decisions about what I'm wearing
No more racing the clock to get everything done

No more anger and deceit
No more addictions left to beat
No more killing no more stealing
No more violence on our streets
No more abuse neglect and doom
No more of our babies to die too soon

Sounds like Heaven to me
Sounds like Heaven to me
Our new homes in Heaven will be
sure sounds like Heaven to me

STARTING OVER

Listen to a story about
    a gal named Deb
She started all over
losing most of what she had

She kept it all together
and didn't ever look back
She found herself again
now look at where she is at

I'm on recovery road
and soon I will arrive
I have to be persistent
if I am going to survive

I'll get back on the saddle
and I'll hold on for the ride
I know I'm going to make it
because God is on my side

STILL TIME FOR YOU

Do you ever wonder what happens when we die
Have you heard the Story of Creation
Who Jesus is and why He died
God sent His only Son to pay the price for Sin
Do not worry there's still time for you

This Book The Holy Bible with Instructions and our guide
with all the key ingredients You'll want to read inside
Both the Old and New Testaments are written there for you
As you continue to read you will surely see

How closely this Book will relate to you and me
God offers us free-will It's a simple yes or no
We'll all be held accountable for the choices we've made
If your heart is racing and feeling some concern
Do not worry there's still time for you

Our Father God in Heaven He does care
He wishes no one to perish It's our job to help and share
God will acknowledge a sorrowful repentant heart
He knows our every intention He hears your every prayer

When Jesus knocks on your Hearts' door
Accept Him as your Lord and Savior
It's only by His Amazing Grace
We shall have Eternal Life after once we die
Do not worry there's still time for you

TEARDROPS

My teardrops fall like
pouring rain from some
these old memories
I wish no longer to contain

The painstaking sorrows are
filled with yesterday's horrors
The pains run deep
into my troubled soul

I know I must let these go
holding on to yesterday's sorrows
I can't move on to a brighter tomorrow

I want to do better
I keep trying to get it right
I still slip and fall
I keep running into walls

God has wiped my slate clean
my tears have all dried
He wants you to know
you've got to let them go

THANKFUL

I am thankful for all things big and small
for our world, He created knowing it would fall
For the air we breathe for the winds that
wrestle the leaves in the trees

I am thankful for God's Promises
I can do anything I put my mind to
and even more thankful that
God's Word will always hold true

I am thankful for our
amazing bodies He designed
and the outstanding compliment
of a sound secure mind

I am thankful for the Blood of Jesus
that cleanses me from sin
Blessed by the Holy Spirit
that lives and reigns from within.

The most important thing
I am thankful for
One day I'll reside in Heaven
with Him forevermore

CPSIA information can be obtained
at www.ICGtesting.com
Printed in the USA
FSHW021905121219